Unlock Your Inner Leader

Advanced Communication Techniques for Success

Table of Contents

1. Introduction 1

2. Unlocking Your Leadership Potential 2

    2.1. Defining Your Leadership Style 2

    2.2. Harnessing Emotional Intelligence 3

    2.3. Building Communication Skills 3

    2.4. The Power of Influence 4

    2.5. Cultivating Resilience and Adaptability 4

3. Mapping Your Communication Style 6

    3.1. Understanding Your Current Style 6

    3.2. Getting Feedback 6

    3.3. Communication Style Quadrants 7

    3.4. Adjusting Your Style 7

    3.5. Practicing Active Listening 7

    3.6. Non-Verbal Communication 8

    3.7. Dealing with Difficult Conversations 8

4. The Art and Science of Emotional Intelligence 9

    4.1. Defining Emotional Intelligence 9

    4.2. Emotional Intelligence in Practice 10

    4.3. The Role of Emotional Intelligence in Leadership 11

5. Cultivating Effective Listening Skills 13

    5.1. Understanding the Concept of Effective Listening 13

    5.2. Empowering Your Leadership with Empathetic Listening . . . 14

    5.3. Overcoming Barriers to Effective Listening 14

    5.4. The Profound Impact of Effective Listening on Leadership . . 15

    5.5. Implementing Effective Listening Techniques in
Leadership 15

    5.6. Conclusion 16

6. Framing Powerful Persuasive Messaging 17

6.1. Understanding Your Audience 17

6.2. Crafting The Message 18

6.3. Principles of Persuasion 18

6.4. Connecting Through Storytelling 19

6.5. Delivering Your Message 19

7. Leading Difficult Conversations with Grace 20

7.1. The Art of Difficult Conversations 20

7.2. Effective Listening 21

7.3. Constructive Criticism 21

7.4. Preempting Defensive Reactions 21

7.5. Managing Emotions 22

7.6. Negotiation and Agreement 22

8. Mastering the Art of Non-Verbal Communication 24

8.1. Uncovering the Non-Verbal Cues 24

8.2. Harnessing the Power of Non-Verbal Communication 25

8.3. An Adaptive Approach to Non-Verbal Communication 25

8.4. Conveying Powerful Non-Verbal Signals 26

9. Creating High-Impact Presentations for Influence 28

9.1. Understanding Your Audience 28

9.2. Craft Your Message 28

9.3. Structuring Your Presentation 29

9.4. Embed Engaging Content 29

9.5. Practice, Practice, Practice 30

9.6. Handling Questions and Feedback 30

10. Building Strong Relationships through Communication 31

10.1. Cultivating Active Listening Skills 31

10.2. Building Trust through Open Dialogue 32

10.3. Utilizing Assertive Communication 32

10.4. Non-Verbal Communication in Relationship-Building 33

10.5. Constructive Conflict Resolution 33

10.6. Facilitating Effective Team Communication 34

11. Culminating Skills: Your Personal Leadership Communication Plan 35

11.1. STEP ONE: Self-Assessment 35

Chapter 1. Introduction

Welcome to an empowering journey towards leadership! This Special Report, titled "Unlock Your Inner Leader: Advanced Communication Techniques for Success", is your key to unearthing and harnessing the latent leadership skills within you. Imagine becoming a master communicator, leveraging the power of words and interactions to shepherd teams, inspire results, and skyrocket business success! High-tech jargon? None of that here! This report is filled with practical, easy-to-understand strategies, illustrating how effective communication can transform not just your professional life, but personal experiences as well. So, get ready! By purchasing this special report, you're about to unlock a dynamic, refreshing, and certainly life-enhancing knowledge that's geared to motivate you into becoming the compelling leader you're destined to be.

Chapter 2. Unlocking Your Leadership Potential

In the realm of leadership, theorists have argued there are as many styles as there are leaders, each reflecting the unique combination of skills, personality traits, and experiences the individual brings to the role. To truly unlock your leadership potential and thrive, you must first embark on a purposeful journey of self-discovery and personal growth. This journey must tackle a range of topics from leadership styles, emotional intelligence, communication skills, the power of influence, to resilience and adaptability.

2.1. Defining Your Leadership Style

Initiating your path towards developing your unique leadership style starts with understanding different leadership theories and styles. Scholars have painstakingly studied leadership and presented various theories over the years, such as Transformational Leadership, Servant Leadership, and Authentic Leadership, among others. While it's insufficient to mimic these styles petrified, reflecting upon them will give you a foundation upon which to build your leadership style.

Researching these leadership types, familiarizing yourself with the characteristics of each, and reflecting on their applicability to your persona will set the stage for personalized leadership. It's also crucial to remember that leadership is not a one-size-fits-all injunction. It's contingent on myriad variables such as the nature of the team, organizational culture, immediate challenges, and strategic goals. Therefore, being fluid and adaptable with your leadership style is also a prerogative to effective leadership.

2.2. Harnessing Emotional Intelligence

Leadership is not just about decision making, strategizing, and managing resources - it's significantly about people. Emotional Intelligence (EI), which encapsulates the ability to understand both your emotions and those of others, is indispensable for a leader.

Humans are emotional beings, which influences their motivation, productivity, engagement, and interpersonal relationships. Through emotional intelligence, a leader can navigate these highly human facets of a team or organization. A leader with high EI can discern team members' feelings and perspectives, demonstrate empathy, manage their emotions, and productively channel team emotions towards shared objectives.

Tabulate your emotional strengths and weaknesses through self-reflection exercises, feedback from others, or psychological assessments like the Emotional Intelligence Appraisal test. Focus on areas such as self-awareness, self-management, social awareness, and relationship management.

2.3. Building Communication Skills

Communication forms the bedrock of effective leadership. As a leader, your role is not just limited to imparting decisions, directives, and updates but also involves listening and understanding. Achieving this dual communication trajectory forms the cornerstone of effective leadership communication.

Sharpening your communication skills involves both the "how" and the "what". The "how" connects to your delivery - being clear, concise, respectful, and empathetic. The "what" concerns the content you communicate, such as your vision, objectives, expectations, and feedback. Remember that communication is not a monologue but a dialogue; hence fostering an open communication culture, where feedback and ideas are encouraged, is vital.

2.4. The Power of Influence

Leadership is incomplete without the power of influence. This extends beyond authority; it's about inspiring and persuading your team towards shared goals. Influence stems from a combination of credibility, trust, and rapport with your team, and your ability to articulate a compelling vision.

Credibility and trust are earned, not bestowed, and hinge on your consistency, integrity, and transparency. They are won gradually but can be lost instantly, so it's paramount to safeguard them tenaciously. Meanwhile, building rapport with your team thrives on your earnest interest in their professional growth and personal well-being.

Articulating a compelling vision is about 'selling' a future state that is not only appealing but also realistic and inclusive. Team members are more likely to rally behind a vision they can resonate with and one where they perceive a sense of belonging and contribution.

2.5. Cultivating Resilience and Adaptability

Leadership is often a high-pressure mandate, interspersed with a myriad of challenges and uncertainties. Resilience and adaptability go hand in hand as key attributes to safeguard your leadership vitality amidst these pressures.

Resilience is your ability to maintain a level head, stay the course, and bounce back from setbacks. Embrace mindfulness practices and a positive mindset to strengthen your resilience. Adaptability, on the other hand, is your ability to adjust and improvise. Practice stepping out of your comfort zone and being open to new ideas and approaches to foster adaptability.

No one said leadership is a breezy endeavor; it demands undeterred dedication, commitment, and continuous learning. But once you crack the code of unlocking your leadership potential, the rewards are immensely gratifying. Your renewed journey begins now!

Chapter 3. Mapping Your Communication Style

Employing a more thorough understanding of your articulation style is the first stride in augmenting your leadership capabilities. Through identifying your style, you can tailor your conversations, overcoming communication obstacles, and relating well with your team, ultimately fostering an environment of trust and productivity.

3.1. Understanding Your Current Style

Prior to modifying the way you interact, you must first delve into your existing communication style. To denote your style, pay close attention to how you express yourself on a daily basis, particularly in stress-laden scenarios. Be attentive to your proclivity towards being straightforward or subtle, passive or assertive, verbose or succinct. It can also be beneficial to note if your communication aligns with function (sharing information) or emotion (sharing feelings).

A practical way to tackle this is to keep a communication log. For a week, write down challenging communications, noting the context, your reactions, your type of communication (i.e., verbal, non-verbal, written), and the outcome. This will start to reveal your dominating style.

3.2. Getting Feedback

Acquiring an accurate image of your communication style entails not just self-reflection but also gathering insights from others. Team members or colleagues could provide valuable feedback, informing you about areas needing improvement that remained unnoticed.

You can solicit this feedback via structured surveys or informal discussions. Make sure to reassure them their opinions are valued and will be used constructively.

3.3. Communication Style Quadrants

To streamline this process, communication styles can be sorted into four quadrants: Analytical, Intuitive, Functional, and Personal. Analytical communicators prefer real numbers and data, often kept brief and to the point. Intuitive communicators prefer a broader perspective, avoiding too much detail. Functional communicators enjoy detailed, step-by-step instructions, and Personal communicators rely on emotional language and connection-building.

Once you identify which quadrant your style falls into, you can then utilize this data to modify your style to better connect with different audience types.

3.4. Adjusting Your Style

Now that you've identified and gained feedback on your communication style, the next stage is to make adjustments. The target isn't to "fix" your style but to broaden it, becoming more flexible in adapting to diverse scenarios and audiences.

List out key adjustments needed based on your self-assessment and feedback. Then, create an action plan detailing steps on how you will implement these changes. Revisit this action plan regularly, making amendments where necessary.

3.5. Practicing Active Listening

A key attribute of excellent communicators is their ability for active listening. This means not just hearing the words that someone is saying but truly understanding their message and corresponding effectively. Practice being present, showing empathy, providing feedback, and summarizing or paraphrasing what the speaker has relayed.

3.6. Non-Verbal Communication

Remember that communication isn't just about verbal discussion. Non-verbal cues such as body language, facial expressions, and tone of voice can affect the message you're communicating. Aim for your non-verbal signals to align with your verbal messages to avoid confusion.

3.7. Dealing with Difficult Conversations

At times, leaders may face challenging conversations. These can be eased by adopting a calm demeanor, expressing empathy, and focusing on the problem rather than the person. Avoid blame, keep the conversation focused, and conclude with a clear resolution in mind.

By understanding, adjusting, and continuously refining your communication style, you cultivate a strong relationship with your team, improve team dynamics, and boost overall productivity. Undoubtedly, effective communication is an essential part of your leadership toolkit and harnessing this skill can lead you to remarkable success.

Chapter 4. The Art and Science of Emotional Intelligence

Understanding emotional intelligence is the cornerstone of effective leadership. At a high level, emotional intelligence is the ability to understand and manage our own emotions, and those of the people around us. In the context of leadership, possessing emotional intelligence means being aware of how our emotions and actions can affect the people around us, as well as understanding how other people's emotions can influence their actions and the overall dynamics of the team.

4.1. Defining Emotional Intelligence

Emotional intelligence consists of five components: self-awareness, self-regulation, motivation, empathy, and social skills.

1. Self-awareness: This is the ability to understand your own emotions and how they can affect your thoughts and behaviors. Self-aware individuals are mindful of their feelings and how they can impact other people.

2. Self-regulation: This involves controlling or redirecting one's disruptive emotions and impulses and adapting to changing circumstances. Those who excel in self-regulation typically don't allow themselves to become overly angry or jealous, and they don't make impulsive, careless decisions.

3. Motivation: Leaders with a high degree of emotional intelligence are usually motivated. They are willing to defer immediate results for long-term success. They're highly productive, love a challenge, and are very effective in whatever they do.

4. Empathy: This is perhaps the second-most important element of emotional intelligence. Empathy is the ability to understand the emotional makeup of other people and how your words and actions affect others.

5. Social skills: It's usually easy to talk to and like people with good social skills, another sign of high emotional intelligence. Those with strong social skills are typically team players, adept at managing teams and building a network of contacts and connections.

4.2. Emotional Intelligence in Practice

Conscious practice is key to developing emotional intelligence. Here are some practical ways to cultivate these crucial skills:

1. Reflect on your own emotions: Regularly take time to check in with yourself and examine your emotions. Try to identify what you're feeling and why. This can help to increase your self-awareness.

2. Carefully consider your responses: Instead of reacting immediately to what someone says or does, take a moment to think about your reaction. This can help you develop self-regulation and avoid knee-jerk reactions that may not be beneficial.

3. Work on your listening skills: Instead of just waiting for your turn to speak, really listen to what other people are saying. Try to understand their perspective and feelings, which will help you develop empathy.

4. Develop your people skills: Seek to build positive relationships with others, manage conflicts effectively, and inspire and influence people. All of this can help you to enhance your social skills.

4.3. The Role of Emotional Intelligence in Leadership

Emotional intelligence is crucial to effective leadership. Leaders with high emotional intelligence build strong teams because they understand and value their team members' feelings and perspectives. They can also manage and channel their own emotions, which helps them to make rational, informed decisions.

1. Self-awareness in leadership: Leaders who are self-aware understand their strengths and weaknesses. They acknowledge when they have made a mistake and can accept constructive feedback, which sets a powerful example for their team.

2. Self-regulation in leadership: Leaders who can self-regulate create a positive and stable work environment. They don't let stress or high emotions dictate their actions.

3. Empathy in leadership: Empathetic leaders cultivate a team culture of respect and understanding. By understanding and taking into account their colleagues' feelings, they can resolve conflicts effectively, encourage open communication, and help their team members feel valued and understood.

4. Motivation and leadership: When leaders are motivated and passionate, this enthusiasm often spreads to their team members. This can lead to increased productivity, better team morale, and a more positive work environment.

5. Social skills in leadership: Leaders with excellent social skills can build and maintain good relationships with their team members, other managers, and clients. Good people skills can help to resolve conflicts, build a positive team environment, and create strong, fruitful relationships.

Everyone has the potential to increase their emotional intelligence with awareness and practice. It's a journey that requires dedication, but the payoff is worth it. As leaders in our respective fields, let's strive to harness the power of emotional intelligence to foster a better, more empathetic world.

Chapter 5. Cultivating Effective Listening Skills

Listening is more than just something you do passively; it's an active process, vital in communication and leadership. Understanding its importance and mastering the art of effective listening can significantly impact your leadership journey. In this regard, we will be dissecting the concept of effective listening, ways to enhance this skill, its benefits, and practical examples of action.

5.1. Understanding the Concept of Effective Listening

Effective listening is an active process where the listener consciously makes an effort to understand, interpret, and evaluate what they're hearing. It demands focus, concentration, and the desire to understand the speaker's perspective.

Want to gauge how effective a listener you are? Here's a table outlining five levels of listening:

```
|===
| Level | Description

| Ignoring | Not listening at all.
| Pretend Listening | Acting as if you're attentive
while being mentally somewhere else.
| Selective Listening | Hearing only parts of the
conversation that interest you.
| Attentive Listening | Paying attention to the speaker
but not making an effort to understand their
perspective.
| Empathetic Listening | Understanding and sharing the
```

```
feelings of the speaker.
|===
```

If you identified yourself within the first four levels, don't fret: practice makes progress. Aim to migrate to empathetic listening, which is the hallmark of effective listening.

5.2. Empowering Your Leadership with Empathetic Listening

Empathetic listening enables leaders to tap into employees' thoughts and emotions, creating an environment of trust and respect, which builds robust relationships. Strategies to foster empathetic listening include:

- Maintain eye contact. This demonstrates your engagement and encourages the speaker.
- Use affirmative nods and verbal affirmations to show you're actively listening.
- Paraphrase to ensure you have correctly understood the speaker.
- Let the speaker finish their thought before you respond.
- Ask probing questions to seek clarification or more depth.

Remember, the goal is to understand the speaker's emotions and perspective, not just their words.

5.3. Overcoming Barriers to Effective Listening

Even the most committed listener can falter due to various barriers. Overcome these challenges by:

- Reducing environmental distractions: Choose a quiet, comfortable space for conversations.

- Keeping personal biases in check: Suspend judgments and try to understand the speaker's standpoint.

- Avoiding premature conclusions: Don't jump to conclusions; allow the speaker to complete their thoughts.

- Battling impatience: Keep your focus on the conversation, not on when it will end.

Effective listening isn't easy—it requires practice and a conscious commitment.

5.4. The Profound Impact of Effective Listening on Leadership

Effective listening provides leaders with a deeper insight into problems, helps generate innovative solutions, and enhances teamwork. It fosters an environment where staff feel valued, increasing their motivation, performance and loyalty.

A study by the International Journal of Business Communication found that active empathetic listening positively impacts employee trust and job satisfaction. It concluded that improving managerial listening skills could be a critical way to engage employees effectively, leading to organizational success.

5.5. Implementing Effective Listening Techniques in Leadership

The transition from understanding the importance of effective listening to actual implementation in your leadership journey involves:

- Actively seeking staff feedback: This empowers employees and shows that you value their opinions.

- Encouraging open communication: Foster a culture where employees can share their thoughts honestly.

- Practicing patience: Allow people to express their thoughts without interruption.

- Demonstrating empathy: Understand and validate the emotions of your staff.

- Acting genuinely: Authenticity in listening builds trust and boosts the morale of your team.

5.6. Conclusion

Effective listening is a cornerstone of effective leadership. By mastering this skill, you position yourself to lead with empathy, enhance team dynamics, and unlock the full potential of your organization. Remember, it's not just about hearing - it's about understanding. Make effective listening a priority in your leadership journey, and watch as it transforms your personal and professional relationships for the better.

Chapter 6. Framing Powerful Persuasive Messaging

Effectively framing a powerful persuasive message is an indispensable skill for leading, whether you are addressing a team, making a sales pitch, or communicating with clients. This art not only drives others to respond to your call to action, but it sparks curiosity, fosters empathy, and nourishes trust. Let's embark on an in-depth exploration of creating persuasive messages.

6.1. Understanding Your Audience

The first step to persuasive messaging is understanding your audience. Knowing who they are is vital as it lets you tailor your message to ensure it resonates with them.

Start by defining your audience – considering their demographics, social status, professional background, hobbies, and interests. Also, consider what they value, what motivates them, and what turns them off. This will help you create a message that not only gets their attention but also influences their behavior.

Use empathy maps to get into your audience's shoes. An empathy map is a tool that helps understand an individual or group's needs. It divides your audience's profile into what they say, think, do, and feel. This tool can give you a more comprehensive view of your audience's mindset, which you can use to craft your message.

Example:

```
|=======
|Say |Think |Do |Feel
|'I want to save for retirement.' |'Investing is too
risky.' |Avoids investment opportunities. |Fearful of
```

```
being financially unstable.
|========
```

6.2. Crafting The Message

After you understand your audience, it's time to craft your message. Your message should be clear, concise, consistent, and tailored to your audience's needs. Your words should invoke emotions that align with your audience's values and aspirations. People are more likely to take action if they feel emotionally connected to a message.

The AIDA model is an effective tool for crafting persuasive messages. AIDA stands for Attention, Interest, Desire, and Action. First, grab the audience's attention with a compelling headline or introduction. Then, arouse their interest by explaining the benefits of your offer. Create desire by making the solution personal to them. And finally, prompt them to action with an irresistible call to action.

6.3. Principles of Persuasion

Dr. Robert Cialdini's principles of persuasion can be instrumental in designing your persuasive message.

Reciprocity: Give something before expecting something in return. This could be tangible, like free samples, or intangible, such as sharing valuable insights or encouragement.

Scarcity: People tend to desire what's limited or soon to be less available. Emphasize the uniqueness of your offer or the urgency to act upon it.

Authority: Show subject matter expertise or bring in experts' opinions to increase your credibility.

Consistency: Humans like consistency and will exert effort to maintain it once a commitment is given. Nudge your audience to make a small commitment first; subsequent larger commitments will follow more easily.

Social Proof: We are more likely to engage in behaviors that we see others performing, especially the ones we consider our peers.

Liking: People are more persuasive to those they like. Create likability through similarity, compliments, and cooperative efforts.

6.4. Connecting Through Storytelling

Stories can create powerful connections by engaging emotions, enhancing understanding, and inspiring action. When you integrate storytelling with your persuasive message, it becomes more relatable and memorable. Follow a simple structure for your story: setup, conflict, and resolution.

6.5. Delivering Your Message

The method you choose to deliver your message can significantly impact its effectiveness. Whether you deliver your message verbally in a meeting, or in writing, through an email or a blog post, ensure it's structured and easy to comprehend.

In summary, crafting powerful persuasive messages requires a clear understanding of your audience coupled with strategic message development. Incorporating principles of persuasive psychology and storytelling can make your message more resonating. However, always ensure your message is ethical, truthful, and aligned with your core values.

Chapter 7. Leading Difficult Conversations with Grace

In a leadership role, uncomfortable and high-stakes conversations are inevitable. Regardless of profession, industry, or job title, everyone encounters difficult conversations. What defines you, as a leader, is how you handle them with grace and finesse. This chapter provides an in-depth exploration of strategies you can utilize to transform challenging discussions into positive, productive experiences.

7.1. The Art of Difficult Conversations

Engaging in challenging conversations can be an unpleasant task. However, learning to manage them effectively can improve relationships, eliminate misunderstandings and foster a healthy culture within your team or organization. Upholding open dialogue, even when it involves uncomfortable issues, constructs trust and mutual respect between both parties involved. It shows that you value the other person and their point of view, even when their ideas diverge from your own.

Start by preparing for the conversation. Pinpoint the issue at hand, set clear goals about what you wish to achieve, and plan how to broach the topic. Research, fact-checking, and introspection are vital. Understand your position and feelings as well as trying to anticipate the other party's perspective.

The setting you choose, as well as the time and place, also play a role in how the conversation pans out. Choose a neutral location, free from interruptions and provide adequate time for discussion.

7.2. Effective Listening

Effective listening is key to leading difficult conversations. Often, we're so focused on what we're going to say next that we fail to truly comprehend the other person's narrative.

Active listening involves demonstrating that you value the other party's opinion. It encourages trust, reduces tension, and promotes a more open dialogue. Show through your body language that you are fully engaged, reflect upon and paraphrase their statements to confirm your understanding, validate their feelings, and encourage them to offer more input through open-ended questions.

7.3. Constructive Criticism

Delivering bad news or criticism can be especially difficult but is frequently an unavoidable part of leadership. How the news is delivered can greatly impact an individual's morale and their subsequent performance.

Make it clear that your feedback is not personal but focused on behavior or results. Be fact-based, focusing on the issue and not the person. Implement the Praise-Improve-Praise (PIP) model, beginning and ending with more favorable statements. This approach lessens the blow of criticism and leaves room for positive affirmation, promoting motivation rather than stagnation.

7.4. Preempting Defensive Reactions

Leaders must also be ready for defensive reactions. Being criticized, no matter how constructively, can elicit resentment, avoidance, and denial.

Open by reassuring the individual that your intention is to improve the situation and affirm that you value their role and professionalism. Be patient and understanding, yet firm and direct. Remember that maintaining the status quo is often an unconscious reflex in response to discomfort, so presenting change as a beneficial opportunity can be favorable.

7.5. Managing Emotions

Emotions can escalate quickly during difficult conversations, making them even more challenging to handle.

Acknowledge your feelings prior to the conversation. Recognizing your emotions and their triggers can help manage your responses and remain composed.

During the conversation, validate the other person's feelings without getting caught in the apparent emotional drama. It's essential to remain empathetic and level-headed, emphasizing resolution and beneficial outcomes.

7.6. Negotiation and Agreement

Inevitably, some tough conversations will require negotiation. Having a clear goal and knowing your acceptable boundaries are invaluable during these discussions.

Additionally, seek to find common ground. Highlighting shared interests and working towards the same objective can defuse tension and foster agreement.

Once you've reached an agreement, ensure it is understood and accepted by both parties. Explicitly clarify the details of the resolution and the steps put in place to prevent recurrence of the issue.

Approaching and carrying difficult conversations with grace requires honesty, comprehension, empathy, and patience. Through practicing these essential skills, you can effectively transform difficult discussions into occasions for growth and development.

Chapter 8. Mastering the Art of Non-Verbal Communication

Effective leadership often works outside the realm of spoken words, navigating instead through the vast landscape of non-verbal communication. This invisible yet potent tool plays a primary role in expression, direction, and understanding, and mastering its nuances can significantly bolster the effectiveness of your leadership.

8.1. Uncovering the Non-Verbal Cues

Understanding the role of non-verbal communication begins with recognizing its various forms. Here, we'll explore the significant categories:

- Facial expression: The human face resonates with a range of emotions—happiness, sadness, anger, surprise, fear, and disgust. Picking up on these can provide a critical insight into the emotional state of your team members.

- Eye contact: Often, eyes speak louder than words. Sustained eye contact indicates interest and engagement, while an evasive gaze may suggest discomfort or disinterest.

- Body movement and posture: The way an individual positions themselves can paint a vivid picture of their current thoughts and feelings. Open postures suggest receptiveness and ease, while closed postures may hint at defensiveness or reservation.

- Gestures: Hand movements or tics can often reinforce or contradict the message received from words. Observed in isolation, these can be misleading, but when paired with other cues, they proffer valuable context.

- Proxemics: This studies the use of space and physical distance, providing insights into personal comfort zones and revealing the dynamics between different team members.

- Paralinguistics: This concerns elements such as tone, pitch, rhythm, speed, and volume of speech, which often expresses attitudes or emotions.

- Appearance: Dress code, cleanliness, and formality can offer glimpses into a person's self-image, position, and intentions.

8.2. Harnessing the Power of Non-Verbal Communication

Being aware of these non-verbal cues can open up an additional dimension to your leadership communication. Here are a few tactics to better your understanding and application of these signals:

- Observing discreetly: Make it a point to observe your team members during meetings, informal gatherings, or even during intense discussions. Noticing their non-verbal behavior can reveal sentiments they may not express in words.

- Practice active listening: Active listening goes beyond simply hearing spoken words. It entails recognizing and understanding non-verbal cues to fully appreciate the speaker's message.

- Matching and mirroring: Subtly reflecting the non-verbal signals of others can create a sense of mutual understanding and respect, fostering positive relationships.

8.3. An Adaptive Approach to Non-Verbal Communication

Just like the language changes across regions, cultures, and even organizations, so do non-verbal cues. It is critical for a leader to adapt their understanding depending on these various factors.

- Cultural variations: Different cultures interpret non-verbal cues differently. For instance, in some cultures, intense eye contact is seen as an indication of trustworthiness, while in others, it's considered intrusive and disrespectful.

- Contextual interpretation: Non-verbal clues should not be taken at face value, and must always be interpreted in context. For instance, crossed arms may mean defensiveness but could also simply indicate that a person is feeling cold.

- Personal interpretations: Each individual has their own set of non-verbal cues. This necessitates getting to know each individual on a personal level, understanding their unique non-verbal language.

8.4. Conveying Powerful Non-Verbal Signals

Your job as a leader is not just deciphering non-verbal communication, it involves conveying potent non-verbal signals yourself.

- Maintain a consistent expression: If your verbal and non-verbal messages align, your communication will be more effective. If they do not, your team will most likely follow the non-verbal over the verbal.

- Establish an open demeanor: Having an open posture, maintaining direct eye contact, and showing genuine smiles will make you more approachable and trustworthy as a leader.

- Respect personal space: Recognizing and respecting others' personal space conveys regard for their boundaries.

- Enhance your paralinguistics: Altering your tone, volume, and speed of speech can make your messages more compelling and easier to comprehend.

In conclusion, an astute leader leverages the power of non-verbal communication to decode unspoken sentiments and to send powerful signals of their own. By mastering this art, you can strengthen your rapport with your team, enhance the effectiveness of your communication, and lead with greater impact.

Chapter 9. Creating High-Impact Presentations for Influence

The ability to deliver high-impact presentations is a critical skill for anyone wishing to exert influence and emerge as a leader. In this respect, it's not just about sharing information, but about connecting with your audience, controlling the message, and creating an environment conducive for change and action.

9.1. Understanding Your Audience

Before creating your presentation, it's important to understand your audience. Who are they? What are their needs and expectations? These are critical questions to consider, serving as the foundation of your presentation's design. Consider their background, their expectations, and their language preference.

For example, if you're presenting to a technical audience, they may expect various jargon and technicalities. On the other hand, a non-technical audience might prefer a simplified explanation. Cater your content to your audience's needs and comfort level to hold their attention and convey your message effectively.

9.2. Craft Your Message

Once you've understood your audience, the next step is crafting your message. Start with the end in mind: What action do you want your audience to take from your presentation? Once this is clear, you can frame your talking points and supporting information around it.

Remember to keep your message concise and hassle-free. A well-delivered message is one that's clear, concise, and impactful—resonating well with your audience and holding their attention throughout.

9.3. Structuring Your Presentation

A well-structured presentation wields the power to keep your audience engaged and retain critical information. Here's a proven structure you can use:

1. Introduction - Aim to captivate your audience's attention with a powerful introduction. This could be a compelling story, a startling statistic, or even a thought-provoking question. State your presentation purpose and what the audience will gain from listening.

2. Body - The body holds your main points supported with credible data, facts, and anecdotes. For easy navigation, display this using "signposting" language like "firstly," "an important point is," "Additionally," etc.

3. Conclusion - This is your final chance to make an impact. Summarize your key points and reroute back to your purpose. You might consider ending with a call-to-action, a provoking quote, or a powerful statement that reinforces your message.

9.4. Embed Engaging Content

The effectiveness of your presentation doesn't just linger on what you say, but also how you say it. Remember, your aim is to keep the audience engaged throughout, and this demands creative ways of showcasing your ideas. Consider using anecdotes, real-world examples, data visualizations, videos, and even interactive elements like quizzes or polls. These keep the audience attentive and make complex ideas more digestible.

9.5. Practice, Practice, Practice

The key to delivering a high-impact presentation is practice. Practice helps you master your content, improve your delivery, navigate your presentation tools, and tackle impromptu questions with finesse. Timing is also a vital aspect. People often drift off when a presentation is too long. Practicing also helps you fit your presentation into an allotted time frame.

9.6. Handling Questions and Feedback

Finally, your ability to handle questions and feedback affects how your audience perceives you as a leader. Rather than seeing questions as a challenge, view them as an opportunity to engage and impress your audience with your knowledge and insight. Practice active listening, remain composed, and be sure to respond in a respectful and informed manner.

Remember, a presentation isn't an information dump, but a means of sharing a message. As a leader, it's your chance to connect with and influence your audience. Whether it's to encourage, inspire, or inform, your ability to create high-impact presentations can influence your trajectory toward leadership. And with everything mentioned, we hope you're well-equipped to do just that!

In the next section, we'll be discussing "Managing Difficult Conversations," another paramount aspect of advanced communication influencing your ascent into leadership. Stay tuned!

Chapter 10. Building Strong Relationships through Communication

Effective communication is the lifeblood of strong relationships, particularly in the realm of leadership. Whether cementing bonds with team members or nurturing trust with stakeholders, the power of skillful dialogue can't be understated. Beyond words, communication also encompasses tone of voice, body language, and even silence. This chapter dissects the intricacies of communication in relationship-building, offering tangible strategies to leverage for leadership success.

10.1. Cultivating Active Listening Skills

Active listening is the underpinning of effective conversation. More than just hearing words, it involves understanding intent, acknowledging emotions, and empathizing with the speaker's perspective. Available research confirms that leaders who excel at active listening are often more successful.

Follow these steps to become an active listener:

1. Maintain Eye Contact: This assures the speaker that your focus is solely on the conversation.

2. Nod Occasionally: This non-verbal communication indicates you understand.

3. Provide Feedback: Paraphrase the speaker's words to validate comprehension.

4. Don't Interrupt: Allow the speaker to fully communicate their

thoughts without interruption.

5. Ask Clarifying Questions: This shows your engagement and helps avoid misunderstandings.

10.2. Building Trust through Open Dialogue

Trust is cornerstone to any strong relationship. To build trust, leaders must uphold transparency and openness, particularly when communicating. Here are some strategies:

1. Speak Honestly: Be open about your thoughts, ideas, and feelings.

2. Acknowledge Others' Perspectives: Consider everyone's input valuable and worth hearing.

3. Share Relevant Information: Informational transparency reduces uncertainty and bolsters trust.

4. Reflect: Think about your words and actions, ensuring they reflect your integrity.

10.3. Utilizing Assertive Communication

Assertive communication is a balance between passive and aggressive communication. Assertive communicators respect their own rights and feelings, while also considering the rights and feelings of others.

To become an assertive communicator, remember these pointers:

1. Clarify and Express: Speak about your needs and feelings clearly without blaming others.

2. Maintain Calm: Even when circumstances are challenging, stay

composed.

3. Good Posture: Maintain an open, confident posture.

4. Be Respectful: While articulating your point, respect others' opinions.

10.4. Non-Verbal Communication in Relationship-Building

Nonverbal cues often convey more information than words. It's crucial to be aware of these signals and the messages they send to ensure constructive communication. Consider:

1. Facial Expressions: These can reveal emotions influencing communication.

2. Gestures & Body Language: Be mindful of movements and postures, they can convey attitudes and feelings.

3. Proxemics or Personal Space: Keeping respectful distance can demonstrate respect.

4. Time Management: Punctuality and time management skills can indicate reliability and respect.

10.5. Constructive Conflict Resolution

Conflicts are inevitable in any organization. However, effective communication ensures they act as catalysts for growth.

Conflict resolution strategies:

1. Listen to Understand: Aim to understand the problem first.

2. Keep Emotions in Check: Stay calm and manage your emotions.

3. Prioritize Resolution: Keep focus on problem-solving, rather than asserting dominance.

4. Seek Support if Necessary: Don't hesitate to draw on neutral third-parties to mediate.

10.6. Facilitating Effective Team Communication

Research indicates that high-performing teams communicate effectively. They share a common vision and are unafraid of healthy disagreement.

Here are ways to enhance team communication:

1. Encourage Openness: Cultivate a culture where everyone feels heard.

2. Use Collaboration Tools: Utilize technology to streamline communication and collaboration.

3. Regular Feedback: Regular individual and team feedback sessions can enhance performance.

4. Set Clear Expectives: Clarity on roles and responsibilities can prevent misunderstandings.

In conclusion, strong relationships are pivotal in leadership. Grounded in effective communication, these relationships can transform teams, instigate improvement, and drive business success. As this chapter elucidates, key communication strategies such as active listening, open dialogue, assertiveness, non-verbal signals, conflict resolution, and team facilitation skills play integral roles. By implementing these techniques, leaders can unlock greater heights of success while forging deeper, more meaningful connections with their teams.

Chapter 11. Culminating Skills: Your Personal Leadership Communication Plan

Developing a personalised leadership communication plan is not merely about discovery; it's about fine-tuning your existing abilities, learning new strategies, and mastering the techniques. This comprehensive chapter will serve as a reference guide in forging your unique approach to leadership through advanced compilation of communication techniques.

11.1. STEP ONE: Self-Assessment

Before instituting your leadership communication plan, it's crucial to embark on self-awareness. What are your current communication strengths and areas that require improvement? This understanding will help in shaping your path. Consider evaluating yourself on skills such as listening, emotional intelligence, non-verbal communication, written communication, public speaking, and meeting facilitation, among others.

Strengths	Areas for Improvement

| Listening | Public Speaking

The above table is a sample on how you can assess yourself. Self-assessment provides a clear vantage point on the communication abilities you'll leverage and those you'll aim to enhance.

=== STEP TWO: Identification of Goals

After self-assessment, the next on the agenda is goal setting. Your communication goals should align with your desired leadership outcomes. It's crucial to set targets that define the leader you aspire to be in terms of verbal exchange while providing indicators to measure progress. For example, you may desire your communication style to foster an inclusive environment. The indicators could be improved team trust and mutual respect.

=== Step THREE: Learning New Skills and Techniques

By now, you are aware of your areas for improvement and have set the communication goals. The next step is to acquire new skills and techniques to bolster your leadership communication. Various lifelong learning resources offer skills-training including workshops, digital learning platforms, books, and webinars. Identify reliable resources to suit your learning style.

=== STEP FOUR: Developing a Personalised Communication Style

Leadership communication is not a one-size-fits-all. Successful communication hinges on authenticity; it should represent who you truly are as a leader. Your communication style becomes a reflection of your values, motivations, and outlook. This step involves incorporating your learnt skills and linking them to your authentic self.

For example, if transparency and empathy are your key values, you could practice open communication, allowing yourself to be vulnerable enough to share personal stories with your team, fostering a relationship built on trust.